Today is Guru Nanak's Birthday. It's a special day! My family and I are going to the gurdwara, our temple, to pray.

Here is my picture of Guru Nanak. I'll tell you about him.

Nanak lived in India. When he was seven years old, Nanak went to school and soon learned to read and write.

He was always asking his teachers questions. Sometimes they did not know the answers!

Most of all, Nanak liked to sit quietly and think about God.

3

There are many stories about Nanak.

One day, Nanak was looking after his father's cows. The sun was so hot that he fell asleep.

A snake spread his hood to shade Nanak's face. As Nanak's father came near, the snake slipped away without hurting Nanak.

People thought Nanak was special.

Nanak had two special friends called Bala and Mardana. The boys called each other 'Bhai', which means 'Brother'.

Nanak said everyone should live like brothers and sisters.

One day, Nanak's father gave him some money to spend wisely in the city. On the way, Nanak saw some holy men who were very hungry. He spent his money on food for them.

His father was angry!

When he grew up, Nanak washed in the river every morning then said his prayers to God.

One day, Nanak went to the river to wash but did not come home. His friends were very worried about him.

After three days Nanak came home. He was happy and said God had given him a special job. He had to teach others about God.

Nanak was called Guru Nanak. 'Guru' means 'Teacher'.

Guru Nanak and his friends Bala and Mardana travelled from village to village to teach people about God.

Guru Nanak said that God made everything on earth. God was the Creator of all things and everyone should pray to him.

Sometimes Guru Nanak sang about God and Mardana played his rebeck. Many people came to listen to Guru Nanak's songs.

Guru Nanak told people that they should all be like brothers and sisters.

He said they should tell the truth, work hard, help others and be kind to animals and birds.

Many people loved Guru Nanak. They tried to do the things he taught them.

At the gurdwara today, men and women will be reading our holy book, the Guru Granth Sahib. We will listen and hear some stories about Guru Nanak.

My mum, my dad and I will sing some songs then go to the langar, our special dining-room, to share some food with friends.

Everyone is happy on Guru Nanak's Birthday!

15

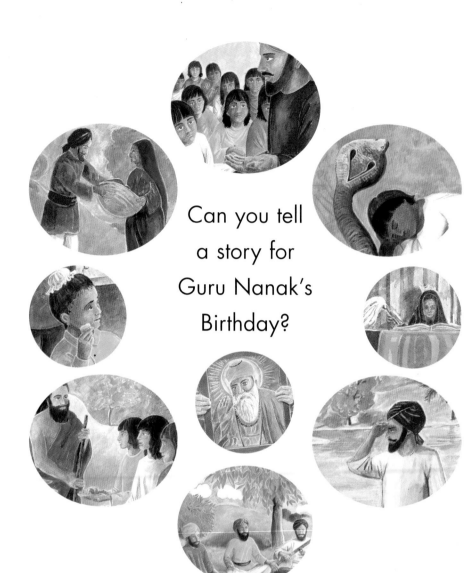

Can you tell a story for Guru Nanak's Birthday?

Published by Religious and Moral Education Press, A division of SCM-Canterbury Press Ltd, St Mary's Works, St Mary's Plain, Norwich, Norfolk NR3 3BH

Copyright © 1999 Lynne Broadbent and John Logan. Lynne Broadbent and John Logan have asserted their right under the Copyright, Designs and Patents Act, 1988, to be identified as Authors of this Work.

All rights reserved. First published 1999. ISBN 1 85175 185 8

Designed and typeset by Topics – The Creative Partnership, Exeter. Printed in Great Britain by Brightsea Press, Exeter for SCM-Canterbury Press Ltd, Norwich